*it**books***

Illustrations on pages 20-1, 24-5, 38-9, 42-3, 58-9, 62-3, 80-1, 86-7, 94-7, 116-7, 122-3 © Headcase Design 2009.

Dancing in the Street (1964) by Martha and the Vandellas. Written by William Stevenson and Marvin Gaye.

FIRST EDITION

Designed by Headcase.
Illustrations on pages 20-1, 24-5, 38-9, 42-3, 58-9, 62-3, 80-1, 86-7, 94-7, 116-7, 122-3 by Headcase Design.
Additional illustrations by Stefanie Coltra.

Library of Congress Cataloging-in-Publication Data has been applied for.

ISBN-13: 978-0-06-188180-0

Conceived and produced by
Elwin Street Limited
144 Liverpool Road
London N1 1LA
www.elwinstreet.com

Printed in China

BUST A MOVE

Six Decades of Dance Crazes

J.K. Manero

AN IMPRINT OF **HarperCollins** PUBLISHERS

C O N T E N T S

PEOPLE HAVE BEEN GETTING DOWN AND GROOVY for millennia. Ever since early man first emerged squinting from their caves, gathered together on a clear patch of grass, and in one voice yelled, "Spin me a tune, DJ!," mankind has felt the need to twist, gyrate, and jump to a beat. It's human nature, a calling that we feel whenever the tune is banging and the mood is right.

Just because dancing is hardwired into our DNA, doesn't mean it comes easily to us all. For anyone who's ever worried about having two left feet, or wanted to expand their dance floor repertoire, this book shows you how to bust the main moves from the last six decades, from hand jiving to booty shaking, as well as the best tunes to get moving to. But it doesn't end there. Sure you need the moves and the killer tracks—that's all here, baby—but you can't truly get down on the dance floor without looking the part. Well don't fret, we've got the whole package: No matter what your chosen era, you'll find out all about the perfect outfits to get your groove on in style.

Rock 'n' roll burst onto the scene in the 50s and 60s and gave us the first dance crazes, from the Hand Jive to the Chicken Dance—some of which are still fresh today. Men in

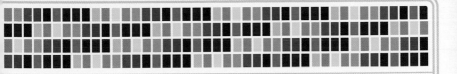

the 50s looked good: They had the wardrobe to match their moves, from rockabilly to the preppy look via James Dean's bad boy denim. And the women looked even better, whether pretty in pink or in poodle skirts.

As the 60s took over, dances like the Twist and the Monkey took off, and the Motown artists showed everyone how to really rock a dance floor. Hemlines got higher as the mini skirt and platform heel combination achived global fame as a signature dance look, alongside hippy chic—think tie-dye with bellbottoms and bandanas to match.

The 70s will live forever as the era of disco funk and dance floor innovation. Disco fostered a whole generation of new dancers that never stopped grooving, and moves like the Hustle remain classics to this day. From Donna Summer to Stevie Wonder, the music was hot, the moves were hotter, and the outfits were practically on fire. With big hair, even bigger flares, and slinky catsuits, they definitely looked the part for flaunting those funky moves.

As the 80s progressed, the music went electronic and dance continued to adapt, from the technical precision of the Robot, through the exhilarating pace of Breakdancing, and the smooth flow of the King of Pop's Moonwalk. People popped,

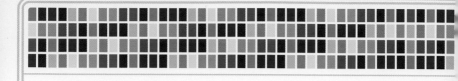

locked, and rocked to the 80s electro beats, and it didn't end there. With the arrival of the 90s, dance lovers went wild to the freeflowing energy of rave and trance, bopped around to bubblegum pop, and grooved to the grungey guitar rhythms of a new generation of musicians. And in the last decade, groovers have been busy shaking their thang to the new hip hop and R'n'B sounds of the 21st century, perfect for the funky precision of Cranking and the energetic Booty Shake.

As the dances evolved, so did the fashion, moving from the 80s flair for big hair and loud suits, through the 90s grunge and rave looks featuring hipster T-shirts and neon glow sticks, to the laidback glamour or full-on bling of the 00s.

The great thing about dancing is that it's all about feeling the groove. It doesn't matter who you are or where you come from, when you get the uncontrollable urge to shake your body, you know you're on to something good. And whether you want to take a trip down musical memory lane or explore some new dance discoveries, everything you need is right here. After reading this book you'll have more moves than a state-of-the-art chess computer, more soul than a glam rocker's day shoe, and more funk than the entire James Brown back catalog.

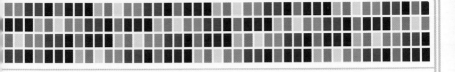

So, it's time to start your journey through dance history and the best routines, sounds, and outfits of the last few decades. Each move has been given a grade based on our disco ball rating system (see key below). To get warmed up, turn to our initial selection of basic moves that anyone can master in minutes. Get the moves, get the tunes, and get the look—it's time to bust a move!

DANCE MOVE DIFFICULTY RATING	
Look for the disco ball rating on each move.	
	Easy steps for anyone with two left feet
	Slightly more complex moves and grooves
	Not for the faint-hearted or the non-flexible

When the music gets going and the dance floor starts filling up, you know it's time to get down and boogie. But are you comfortable twirling the Elvis Pelvis at the right time? Can you body pop to those electro beats with ease? Are you more hop hop than hip hop? Some basic moves are essential to master as a first step. Count these ones as your easy warm-ups for the routines and tougher dance moves to come. Mix them up and make them your own and you'll be well on the way to dance floor nirvana.

Basic Stepping

If you have two left feet but still want to venture out onto the dance floor, then start by stripping it right back and just step in time to the music. With every beat, move one foot sideways and on the next beat bring it back. Then swap feet. You're probably not going to win any dance rosettes, but everyone has to start somewhere. When you're ready to try some more attention-grabbing moves, read on.

Grapevine

The grapevine is a great basic stepping move that can be performed to any tune. Take a step to

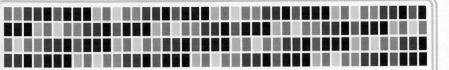

the right with your right foot, then bring your left leg behind it. Take another step with your right foot before bringing your left foot to join it. Clap once as you finish. Repeat in the other direction, starting with your left foot.

Roll the Dough

One for pizza lovers everywhere, try Rolling the Dough to your favorite track. Imitate those Italian masters by clenching your fists and holding out your forearms straight in front of you. With the beat of the music, make little opposing circles with each arm.

Butter Churner

Sticking with the food theme, let's move onto the Butter Churner. Straighten your arms out in front of you with one fist on top of the other. Make circling motions with your arms, like you're churning a vat of butter with a big spoon. Sway from side to side a little for a bit of originality.

The Milker

If rockabilly riffs are your thing then the Milker is a great way to boogie. Have your legs shoulder-width apart, straighten your arms, and stick them out in front of you. Now, pretend you're milking a cow by moving your arms up and down and bending your elbows. The more flamboyant the motions are the better—you don't want to look like a practicing farmhand.

The Pelvic Thrust

When the sweet sound of rock 'n' roll fills the air, gyrate those hips and make The King proud. Elvis

was the master of the pelvic thrust and it's a great basic rock move. Turn your left leg out to the side and bend the knee. Keep your back leg straight. Thrust your hips in the direction of your front leg and to add extra power, bend your back leg as you move.

The Funky Train

For an easy disco move, tuck those elbows into the waist and extend your lower arms in front of you, like you're about to do a double karate chop. Open your palms and move them back and forward like a steam train's wheels. Roll your shoulders with each movement. When you've got that down to a tee, try thrusting your hips in time with the music. You'll be a disco legend in no time!

Basic Disco

To look truly coordinated when dancing to disco beats, you need to have your arms and legs moving in different directions. Stand with your legs shoulder-width apart. Move your left leg across your right leg and at the same time raise your left arm out to the side and loosely cross your body with your right arm. Do the opposite when you cross your right leg over. You need to keep it fast and fluid or you're in danger of looking like a magician.

Travolta Strut

Turn heads as you hit the dance floor, by breaking out your Travolta Strut. As you step, move each foot slightly in front of the other. This will give you a funky gait. Keep in time to the music with each step. As you step with your right foot, roll your right shoulder a little, and the opposite for the left stride. Nod your head to the beat as you walk, for extra flair.

Fishing Line

If you spot someone you like on the dance floor, reel them in. Pretend you're holding a fishing line and cast it out to sea. With the beat of the music, pull back on your line. It's a surefire way to land a dance partner.

The Shimmy

Keep your body still, hold out your arms a little and slightly bend the elbows. Now rock your shoulders back and forth, right forward, left back, left forward, right back etc. Speed it up or slow it down, depending on the speed of the track, or even lower your body to the floor as you do it.

Tootsie Roll

A perfect move for hip hop tunes. Stand with your legs shoulder-width apart and raise yourself up slightly on your toes. Stick your rump out a bit and make butterfly motions with your legs by moving your knees in together and then out to the side.

Raising the Roof

Stretch out your palms and raise them above your head, so they are facing the roof. With the beat of the track make a heavy lifting motion up and down. Sway a little from side to side as you go to look extra fly.

The Arm Worm

For those unable to perform the classic worm—wiggling your entire body along the length of the dance floor—this recreates the motion with your arms. Hold one arm out in front and across your body, bend your wrist and raise your elbow, then flick your wrist back up and lower your elbow. Repeat this movement and gradually move your arm across your body. A look of amazement should be displayed on your face as you do it.

19

50s

Grab your poodle skirts and letter sweaters. It's time to jump and jive to the look and the sounds of the 1950s. Let's learn to do the wildest of all these dances ever.

The 1950s

TEENS IN THE 50s HAD IT MADE when it came to cutting a rug. All sorts of great new music burst onto the scene aimed at this dance-crazed bunch. The world over, kids were breaking out of the conservative mold and pulling on their dancing shoes, ready to go wild to the new tunes of the day. And if they weren't shaking their hips to Elvis they were jumping and jiving to the likes of The Everly Brothers, Jerry Lee Lewis, and Buddy Holly. If you want to live it up 50s style, then put on your blue suede shoes and get ready to shake, rattle, and roll!

THE BIRTH OF ROCK 'N' ROLL

This new generation needed an up-to-date music genre to match, and so rock rolled into town. The strong back-beats and addictive fusion of country music and rhythm and blues made for instant dance floor hits. And with artists like Elvis Presley, Fats Domino, and Jerry Lee Lewis hitting the microphone, it was a super cool sound with even cooler stars.

ROCKING TRACK

For a 50s track that's sure to get all your friends dancing, "Rock Around the Clock" is the perfect number. It was a smash success for Bill Haley and His Comets in 1954.

THE KING

During the 50s a king was born. That king was Elvis Presley. The ultimate 50s musical superstar, he swooned, rocked, and shook up the world with his provocative dancing, catchy tracks, and good looks. The King's look epitomized the fresh new 50s style. His greased-up hair, clean-cut features, black leather jacket, and controversial gyrating hips left women's hearts melting and men trying to copy him . . . many still are!

BANANA BEATS

It wasn't just rock 'n' roll that got people dancing in the 50s. In 1957 Harry Belafonte had everybody swinging to a classic calypso beat with his song "Day-O (The Banana Boat Song)."

AMERICAN BANDSTAND

The 50s was the decade of the television revolution, and dance soon caught up with the act. In 1957 *American Bandstand* hit the air. The program showcased all the latest dance crazes from around the world. Every afternoon, teenagers would turn on the TV and dance the afternoon away. All the best bands played their latest songs, making it *the* place to hear all the top new tunes. The show became so popular with dancers that it even began to generate new and exciting dances itself.

THE
CHICKEN
DANCE

 First, get into character. Tuck your arms up under your armpits and make little wings. Crane your neck out as if you're about to start pecking.

 Flap your wings like you're trying to fly, keeping your movements in time to the beat.

 While still flapping your wings, on the beat extend your right leg backward before bringing it back to the floor on the second. Repeat with your left leg. Don't worry about balance—the more wobbly the better.

Combine your wing flaps and leg extensions with the odd head-peck on your way to becoming the king (or queen) of the barn dance.

People love to dance like poultry. This fad dance was created in the 1950s and later was often combined with the Twist to make one super-move. Other poultry-inspired selections include the Oom-pah dance of the same decade as well as "The Birdie Song" in the 1980s.

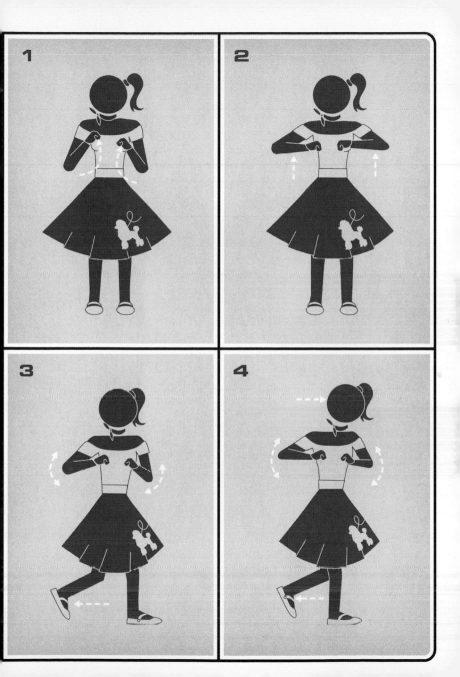

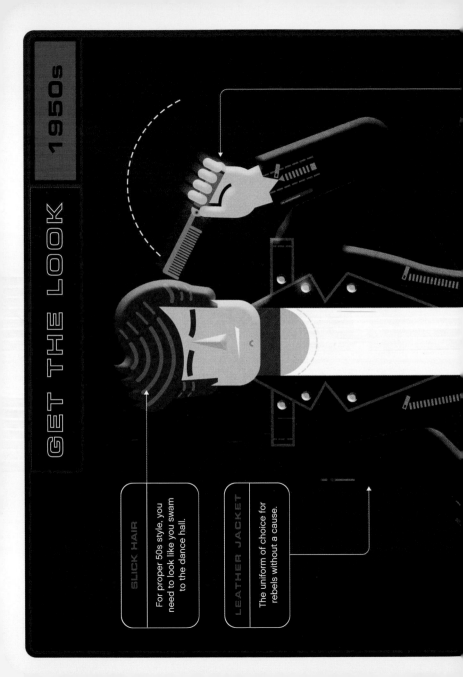

GET THE LOOK

SLICK HAIR

For proper 50s style, you need to look like you swam to the dance hall.

LEATHER JACKET

The uniform of choice for rebels without a cause.

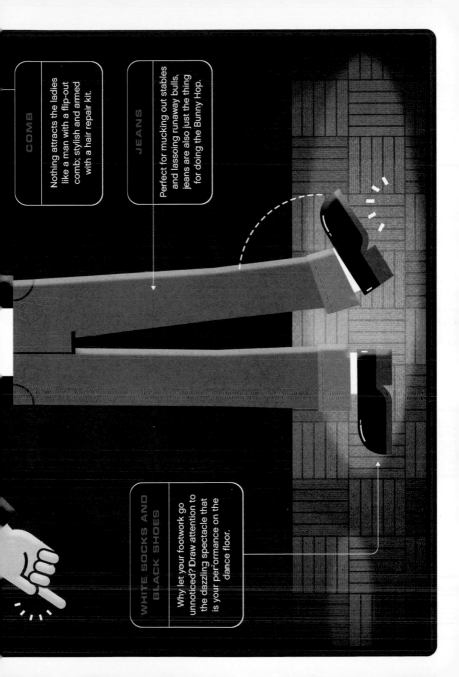

COMB

Nothing attracts the ladies like a man with a flip-out comb; stylish and armed with a hair repair kit.

JEANS

Perfect for mucking out stables and lassoing runaway bulls, jeans are also just the thing for doing the Bunny Hop.

WHITE SOCKS AND BLACK SHOES

Why let your footwork go unnoticed? Draw attention to the dazzling spectacle that is your performance on the dance floor.

THE
HAND JIVE

 Take a trip to coolsville. Start off squatting down slightly with bent legs. Pat your hands on your thighs twice, then clap your hands twice.

 With your arms bent and in front of you at about waist-height, flatten your palms and cross your right hand over your left twice, then cross your left over your right hand twice.

 Bounce those fists—clench your hands and alternate hitting one on top of the other.

Time to hitchhike. Get your thumbs up and, alternating between each arm, raise your hand over your shoulder. The world's your oyster.

You can add all sorts of complicated hand movements to this one. A rock and roll classic, the Hand Jive can be performed solo as shown or with a partner, like a super-cool, sped-up version of patty-cakes. For inspiration, check out the moves performed in the all-time dance classic, Grease.

PONYTAIL

Simple and cute . . . exactly the opposite of the moves you'll be busting.

WAISTLINE

A cinched-in waist creates the perfect hourglass figure, but be careful—no one wants to faint at the sock hop.

NECKERCHIEF

Keep the cute theme going with a neckerchief to leave you looking sweet and refined.

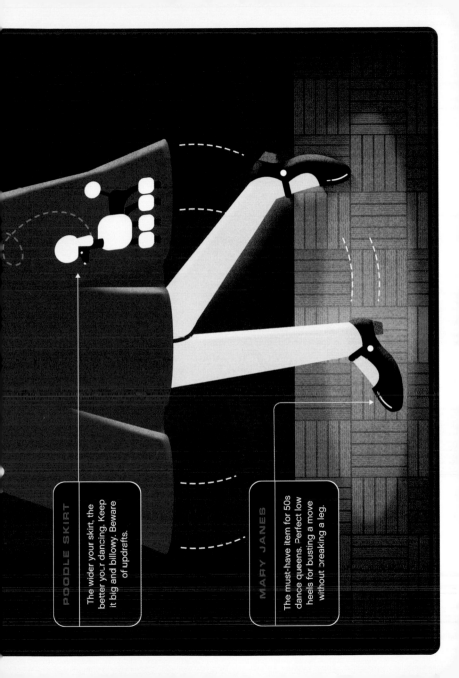

POODLE SKIRT

The wider your skirt, the better your dancing. Keep it big and billowy. Beware of updrafts.

MARY JANES

The must-have item for 50s dance queens. Perfect low heels for busting a move without breaking a leg.

THE
BUNNY HOP

1 You'll need a few friends for this one, standing in a line. Hold onto the person in front of you, with both your hands on their hips. Kick out your right leg, touching your heel on the floor, and bring it back in. Repeat this twice and then do the same with the left.

2 Staying in your bunny line, hop forward and land on both feet.

3 Then, hop backward, landing on both feet. Keep it light and nimble and in time to the beat.

4 With a spring in your step, hop forward three more times with the beat of the music. See how many people you can get to join in.

....

If you've had enough of the Conga, break out the Hop instead. It's a great social mixer dance, created in a San Francisco high school in 1952. Perfect for getting even the shyest dancers onto the floor.

THE
MADISON

 This is a line dance so you'll need to get the dance floor crowd lined up with you. All ready? Step forward with your left foot.

 Now, bring your right foot forward beside your left without putting any weight on it. Clap once. Then step back to same spot with your right foot.

 Move your left foot back and across your right foot without putting any weight on it.

Uncross your legs by moving your left foot back to the left side. Repeat, until you get repetitive strain injury. Just kidding.

continued

....

A real 50s classic, the Madison was a craze that took the dance world by storm. It's usually performed as a line dance with the steps called out as you go. Look out for this inspired dance in Hairspray, *the movie and the musical.*

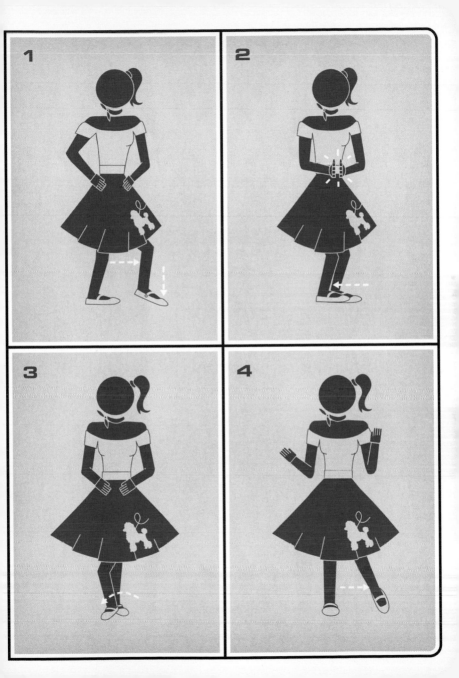

Now you've got the basics, it's time to spice it up a little. Uncross your legs again and, on the spot, hunch over slightly and jog on the spot. When you bring your leg down, cross it over the other one.

End with your legs crossed and your arms up, in rifle-shooting position. We surrender!

ESSENTIAL SOUNDS OF THE 1950s

- **Johnny B. Goode**
  Chuck Berry

- **Jailhouse Rock**
  Elvis Presley

- **Rock Around The Clock**
  Bill Haley & His Comets

- **Tutti-Frutti**
  Little Richard

- **Whole Lot of Shakin' Going On**
  Jerry Lee Lewis

- **What'd I Say**
  Ray Charles

- **Hound Dog**
  Elvis Presley

- **Long Tall Sally**
  Little Richard

- **Bo Diddley**
  Bo Diddley

- **Shake, Rattle And Roll**
  Joe Turner

- **Blue Suede Shoes**
  Carl Perkins

- **Great Balls Of Fire**
  Jerry Lee Lewis

- **Day-O (The Banana Boat Song)**
  Harry Belafonte

- **Be-Bop-A-Lula**
  Gene Vincent & the Bluecaps

- **Rock And Roll Music**
  Chuck Berry

- **Peggy Sue**
  Buddy Holly

- **Please, Please, Please**
  James Brown & the Famous Flames

- **Sh-Boom**
  Chords

- **I Walk The Line**
  Johnny Cash and the Tennessee Two

- **The Great Pretender**
  Platter

- **Sweet Little Sixteen**
  Chuck Berry

- **The Train Kept-A-Rollin**
  Johnny Burnette Trio

- **Let The Good Times Roll**
  Shirley & Lee

- **Rip It Up**
  Little Richard

- **Roll Over Beethoven**
  Chuck Berry

- **Rocket 88**
  Jackie Brenston

- **Rockin Pneumonia and the Boogie Woogie Flu**
  Huey "Piano" Smith & the Clowns

- **All Shook Up**
  Elvis Presley

- **Mack The Knife**
  Bobby Darin

- **Wake Up Little Susie**
  Everly Brothers

- **La Bamba**
  Ritchie Valens

- **I'm Walkin'**
  Fats Domino

- **Shout**
  The Isley Brothers

- **Keep A 'Knockin'**
  Little Richard

- **Kansas City**
  Wilbert Harrison

- **Poison Ivy**
  Coasters

- **Hang Up My Rock And Roll Shoes**
  Chuck Willis

- **At The Hop**
  Danny & the Juniors

- **Good Golly Miss Molly**
  Little Richard

19

60s

Expand your mind and get grooving to the eclectic sounds of the 1960s. Free your soul and let the music take control . . .

- THE MONKEY
- THE TWIST
- THE MASHED POTATO
- THE PONY

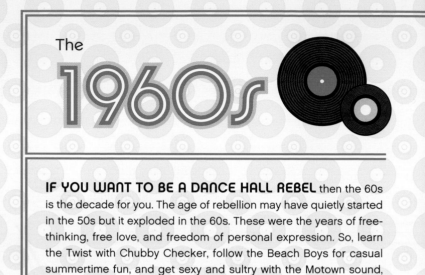

The 1960s

IF YOU WANT TO BE A DANCE HALL REBEL then the 60s is the decade for you. The age of rebellion may have quietly started in the 50s but it exploded in the 60s. These were the years of free-thinking, free love, and freedom of personal expression. So, learn the Twist with Chubby Checker, follow the Beach Boys for casual summertime fun, and get sexy and sultry with the Motown sound, because it's time to get down and groovy, baby, yeah!

THE MOTOWN SOUND

The music label that's so cool it has its own sound, Motown hit the big time in the 60s. And with the creation of high-caliber stars like Diana Ross, Stevie Wonder, Smokey Robinson, the Supremes, and Marvin Gaye, it's no surprise the label has gone down in music legend. "Please Mr. Postman" (1961) by The Marvelettes was Motown's first ever number one smash. Perfect for a slow solo bop or a light boogie with a partner, this great track went on to be be covered by The Beatles and The Carpenters.

SIXTIES SONG

"There'll be swingin', swayin', and records playin' / And dancin' in the streets"

"Dancing in the Street" (1964) by Martha and the Vandellas, is a classic hit, perfect for recreating that soulful 60s vibe. Co-written by Marvin Gaye and William "Mickey" Stevenson, it's one of only a few select songs to be preserved by the Library of Congress. Maybe we'll still be dancing in the streets in a thousand years' time. Unless we're all moonwalking by then.

SUMMER OF LOVE

In 1969, on a dairy farm in Bethel, New York, half a million people came together for one of the coolest music festivals of all time, Woodstock. Performers included Jimi Hendrix, Ravi Shankar, The Who, and Janis Joplin—names that are still world-famous today. Although Joni Mitchell didn't appear, she watched it on TV and wrote the song "Woodstock" to commemorate the festival.

LIVING LEGEND

Stevie Wonder had his first hit aged just 13. "Fingertips Part II" was the start of his glittering career. Play the track and just try not to dance to his harmonica solo. Wonder's legendary status was borne out of songs like "Superstition," which has a bass line so groovy it's sure to get your bones swaying, and "You Are the Sunshine of My Life," perfect for smooching with your partner.

BEATLEMANIA

You may have heard of a little band named The Beatles ... John Lennon, Paul McCartney, Ringo Starr, and George Harrison formed this awesome foursome in 1960, and went on to straddle the decade.

THE
MONKEY

 Time to monkey around. Keep it fresh and improvise. Start off by waving your arms in the air like a playful orangutan.

 While stamping your feet a little, move your arms down and wave them out to the side, rotating your shoulders.

 Try the classic armpit scratch. A monkey facial expression would not be out of place, either.

4 Bobbing your head around, hop up and down on one foot. Repeat with random monkey moves of your choosing. It's a jungle out there.

1963 was the year of the Monkey: "Monkey Time" by Major Lance and "Mickey's Monkey" by The Miracles were both released, and people just had to monkey around to them. For extra fun, do the Monkey with a partner and be as creative as you can with your moves.

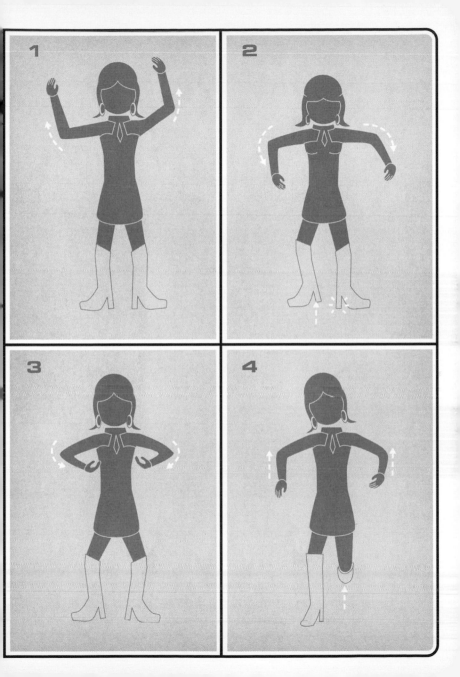

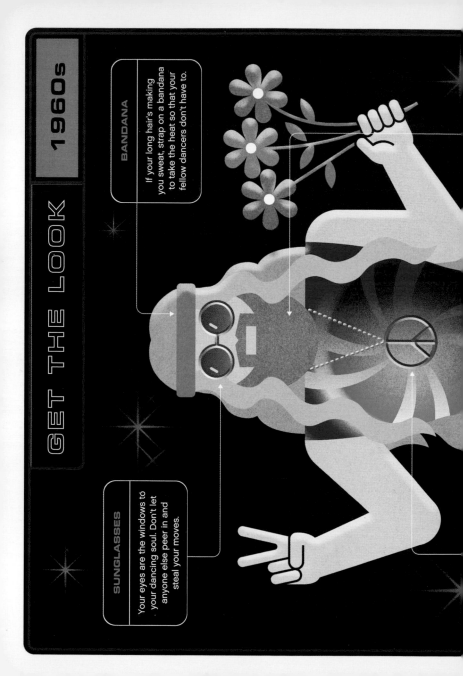

BANDANA

If your long hair's making you sweat, strap on a bandana to take the heat so that your fellow dancers don't have to.

SUNGLASSES

Your eyes are the windows to your dancing soul. Don't let anyone else peer in and steal your moves.

LONG BEARD

For true late-60s style, go for the dance floor yeti look. It will cost you a lot in extra shampoo though.

TIE-DYE SHIRT

Pure psychedelic madness, your shirt should be as mesmerizing as your moves.

PEACE SIGN

What better way to show off your political and ideological beliefs than with a cheap piece of mass-produced jewelry?

BAREFOOT

True hippies don't need shoes. Perfect for wandering through grassy meadows. Less cool if someone treads on your feet.

THE
TWIST

 1 All cool cats need to know how to twist. Stand with your legs shoulder-width apart, clench your fists, and bend your arms by your side.

 2 Start to rotate your hips in time to the music. Move your right leg just in front, rest on your toes, and swivel from left to right with your hips.

 3 As you turn your body to the right, roll your right shoulder and push out your arm a little. Mirror this as you move to the left.

4 For added groove, bend your legs and lower yourself a little as you keep on twisting.

Probably the most popular dance in the world, the Twist is synonymous with Chubby Checker's hit by the same name. The song and the dance hit the big time when it was shown on American Bandstand, proving that sometimes it is a great idea to copy what you see on TV.

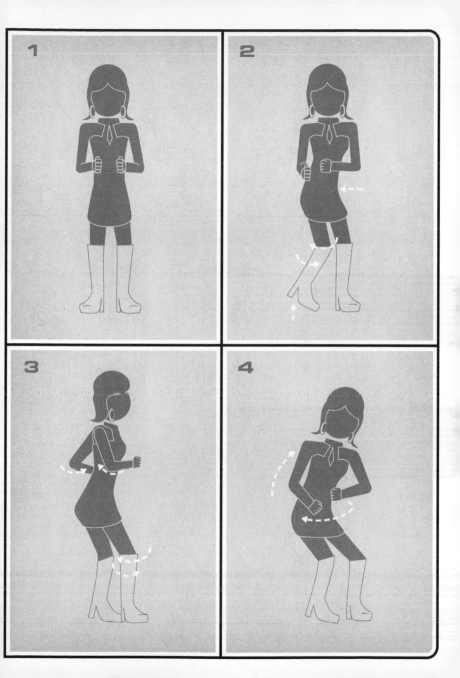

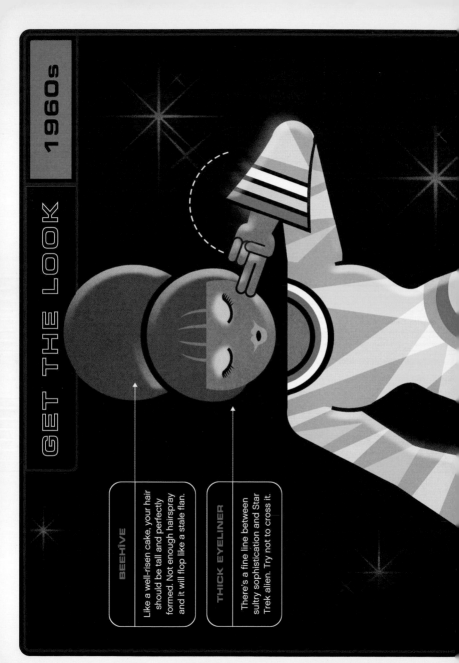

BEEHIVE

Like a well-risen cake, your hair should be tall and perfectly formed. Not enough hairspray and it will flop like a stale flan.

THICK EYELINER

There's a fine line between sultry sophistication and Star Trek alien. Try not to cross it.

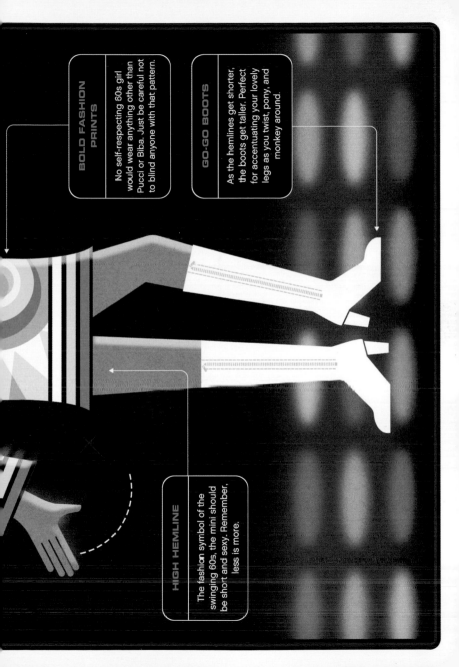

BOLD FASHION PRINTS

No self-respecting 60s girl would wear anything other than Pucci or Biba. Just be careful not to blind anyone with that pattern.

GO-GO BOOTS

As the hemlines get shorter, the boots get taller. Perfect for accentuating your lovely legs as you twist, pony, and monkey around.

HIGH HEMLINE

The fashion symbol of the swinging 60s, the mini should be short and sexy. Remember, less is more.

THE
MASHED
POTATO

1 No kitchen utensils needed. Stand with your legs shoulder-width apart. Bend your knees in a little and lean on your toes slightly.

2 Click your heels together twice with the music. Not three times, this isn't *The Wizard of Oz*.

3 On the second click, shift your balance to your left leg and, keeping the same rhythm, kick your right foot out a little before bringing it back.

4 Click two more times, shift your balance to your right leg, and kick your left leg out a little. It sounds easy but it isn't! Start slowly and speed up gradually to bring this baby to the boil.

Inspired by the Twist, this move seems simple to the untrained eye but give it a whirl and you'll find it more challenging than it looks. To do it right, crank up the volume and play Dee Dee Sharp's "Mashed Potato Time" (1962).

44

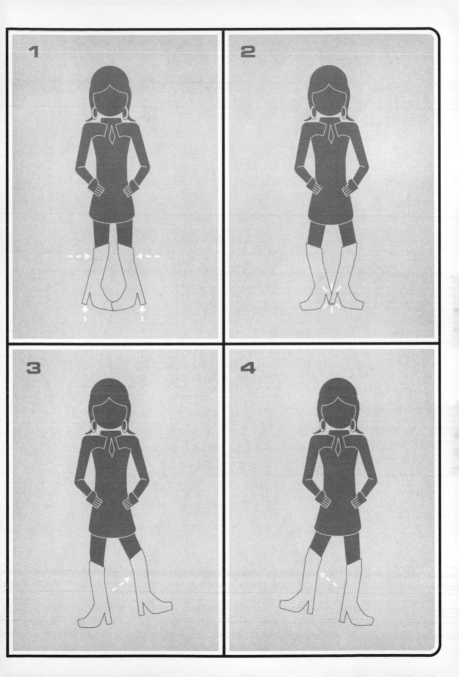

THE
PONY

 Do this on your own or facing a partner. Start by jumping to the right on your right foot; keep your left foot close to your ankle and raised.

 Bring your left foot down to the floor, resting it on your toes and, at the same time, raise your right foot up to ankle height. Do the same with the opposite foot. The odd "neigh" is optional.

3 Repeat step 1 but this time use your opposite leg. Jump to the left with your left foot and keep your right foot suspended beside your ankle.

 Next, bring your right foot down onto your toes and raise your left to ankle height. And do the same with the opposite foot. Repeat over and over, you one-trick pony you.

continued

Another Chubby Checker creation, this move is one for the equine elite. "Pony Time" (1961) is the track to giddy-up and get down to with this sequence. You can even go riding with a partner. Yee-haw!

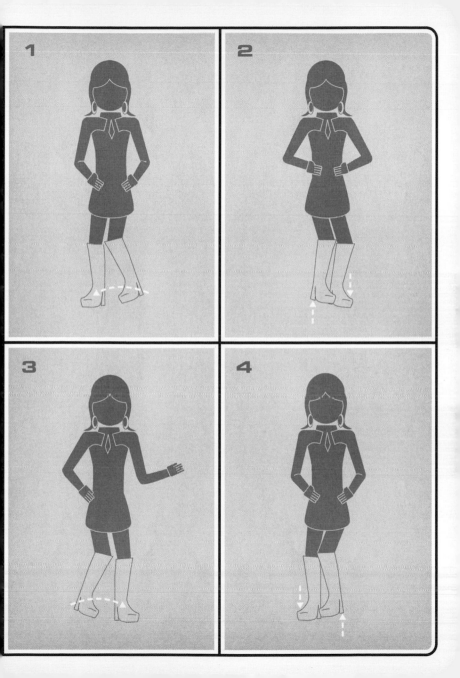

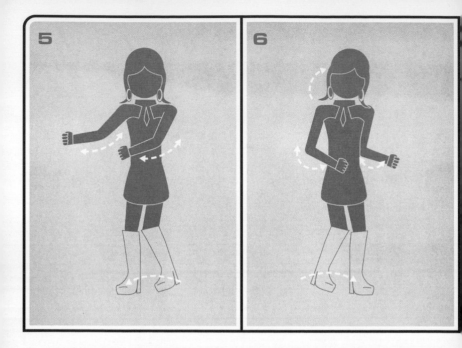

 Now add some arm movements. As you jump to the right, hold out your arms like you're tugging on the reins. Sway a little as you go. Looking good, cowboy.

As you jump to the left, lower your arms to your side, keeping your body swaying and nodding your head to the beat. Giddy up!

ESSENTIAL SOUNDS OF THE 1960s

- **(I Can't Get No) Satisfaction**
  Rolling Stones

- **Respect**
  Aretha Franklin

- **I Heard It Through The Grapevine**
  Marvin Gaye

- **Do You Love Me?**
  The Contours

- **Good Vibrations**
  The Beach Boys

- **Light My Fire**
  The Doors

- **Louie Louie**
  The Kingsmen

- **Dance to the Music**
  Sly and the Family Stone

- **You Really Got Me**
  The Kinks

- **In The Midnight Hour**
  Wilson Pickett

- **Twist and Shout**
  The Isley Brothers

- **Purple Haze**
  Jimi Hendrix

- **Whole Lotta Love**
  Led Zeppelin

- **Georgia On My Mind**
  Ray Charles

- **The Twist**
  Chubby Checker

- **Get Ready**
  The Temptations

- **You Keep Me Hangin' On**
  The Supremes

- **Wild Thing**
  The Troggs

- **The Loco-Motion**
  Little Eva

- **Bristol Stomp**
  The Dovells

- **I'm A Believer**
  The Monkees

- **Dancing In The Street**
  Martha & the Vandellas

- **Harlem Shuffle**
  Bob and Earl

- **Under The Boardwalk**
  The Drifters

- **Land of 100 Dances**
  Wilson Pickett

- **Time Of The Season**
  The Zombies

- **I Got You (I Feel Good)**
  James Brown

- **Papa's Got A Brand New Bag**
  James Brown

- **My Generation**
  The Who

- **Mashed Potato Time**
  Dee Dee Sharp

- **I Want To Hold Your Hand**
  The Beatles

- **I Want You Back**
  Jackson 5

- **Soul Man**
  Sam & Dave

- **I Get Around**
  The Beach Boys

- **Born To Be Wild**
  Steppenwolf

- **Ticket To Ride**
  The Beatles

- **Like A Rolling Stone**
  Bob Dylan

- **California Dreamin'**
  The Mamas & the Papas

- **Nights In White Satin**
  Moody Blues

- **Madison Time**
  The Ray Bryant Combo

70s

In the 1970s disco fever struck the dance halls of the world as men and women strutted their stuff to the funky beats and soulful tunes that filled the air.

- THE HUSTLE
- THE BUMP
- THE BUS STOP
- SATURDAY NIGHT FEVER

The
1970s

HAVE YOU GOT THE FUNK? The 70s was a decade defined by the different offerings on the dance floor, from disco to punk and just about everything in between. As well as disco legends like the Bee Gees and Donna Summer getting down and dirty, the 70s also witnessed a musical masterclass from the likes of Eric Clapton, Bruce Springsteen, and, who could forget, the Village People. So pull on those platforms and strut your stuff like Tony Manero, it's time to get down and party.

DANCE MECCA

Seventies dancers looking for the ultimate in entertainment and no-holds-barred party-mania had only one place to go: Studio 54. This Manhattan funk palace opened its doors in 1977 and offered party-goers a theatrical setting to dance the night away. The fever soon struck and it became a much-loved hangout for the grooviest cats in showbiz. Guests included Andy Warhol, Cher, Liza Minelli, and the future king of pop and dance legend himself, Michael Jackson. In its heyday, no club in the world could outdo Studio 54 for sheer excess and hedonism.

SATURDAY NIGHT FEVER

The soundtrack to this eternally popular movie has sold over 30 million copies worldwide, and many tracks still pack out dance floors today. Read on for the lowdown on how to bust Tony Manero's main moves.

D.I.S.C.O.

Disco was born when super hot DJs began mixing existing tunes with their own samples of instrumental interludes and groovy bass lines. They were an instant hit in the underground dance havens across America and it wasn't long before disco spread around the world. Among the many great artists to get in on the disco scene were Barry White, Gloria Gaynor, and The Jackson Five, who all offered up awesome disco tunes to get down and groove to. Read on to find out just how to recreate those heady days of disco.

DONNA SUMMER

One of the shining lights of the era was disco diva, Donna Summer. Her most memorable tracks are, "Love to Love You, Baby" and "I Feel Love" (the latter pioneered the use of electronic sounds.) Her sultry, sexy stage presence and erotic lyrics matched the image of the emerging disco scene perfectly.

NEW BEATS

The late 70s is where it all began for hip hop, born out of block parties in New York, but with its roots in African music.

THE
HUSTLE

1 It's time to get the disco inferno started. Strut back with four beats of the music, then take four steps forward.

2 Heat things up a little by turning to the right and performing the rolling grapevine by spinning round once and clapping your hands, in time with four beats. Burn that dance floor up.

3 To really get things cookin' do the Travolta point and work those hips to the count of four beats.

4 Lastly, make like an egg-beater, by rolling your arms over each other. Break out the extinguisher, you're on fire!

....

There's only one tune to go for when it comes to showing off these moves. Strut your funky stuff to the "The Hustle" by Van McCoy and the Soul City Symphony (1975).

THE
BUMP

 1 Rock your body to the groovy bass line. On the beat clap your hands together and prepare to bump your rump.

 2 Take a side step toward the person next to you—ideally your partner—and raise your arms just above your head with your elbows out. Prepare for impact.

 3 On the second beat, swing out your hips and make booty-to-booty contact with your partner.

 4 Clap to the next beat and bump with the fourth, repeating the steps above. To vary, why not turn and bump the other way? Groovy.

Disco doesn't get more intimate than the Bump. If you're feeling racy, bump a little lower to the ground or even backside to hip. For the perfect tune try out "Nutbush City Limits" by Ike and Tina Turner (1973) or "Give up the Funk" by George Clinton and Parliament (1976).

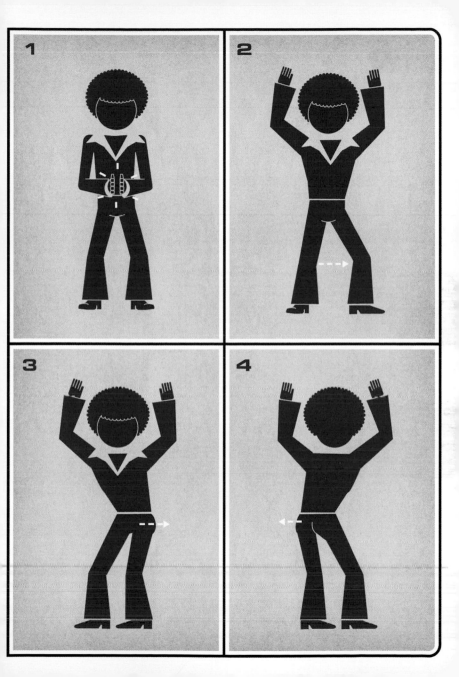

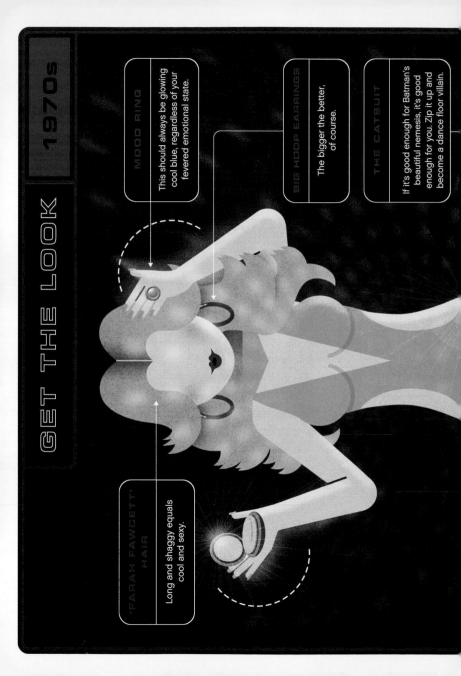

GET THE LOOK

1970s

MOOD RING
This should always be glowing cool blue, regardless of your fevered emotional state.

BIG HOOP EARRINGS
The bigger the better, of course.

THE CATSUIT
If it's good enough for Batman's beautiful nemesis, it's good enough for you. Zip it up and become a dance floor villain.

"FARAH FAWCETT" HAIR
Long and shaggy equals cool and sexy.

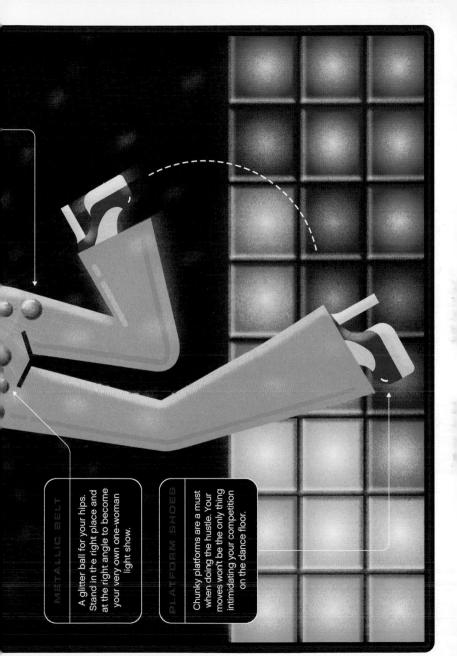

METALLIC BELT

A glitter ball for your hips. Stand in the right place and at the right angle to become your very own one-woman light show.

PLATFORM SHOES

Chunky platforms are a must when doing the hustle. Your moves won't be the only thing intimidating your competition on the dance floor.

THE
BUS STOP

1 Stop looking for a timetable and prepare to boogie. Clap your hands and take three steps back. Then take three steps forward.

2 Next, do the grapevine (see page 10). Standing still, stick your right leg out to the side, and bring it back in, then do the same with your left. Keep your movements in time to the beat.

3 For beats five and six, click your heels together while on your toes—there's no place like home!

4 For the next few beats, bring your right leg forward and back, tapping down on your toes in the process to each.

....

This is another great routine for a line dance, so get everyone involved! Its origins are to be found on the West Coast as it evolved from the Hustle. Keep it simple and boogie to any disco classic from this funkiest of decades.

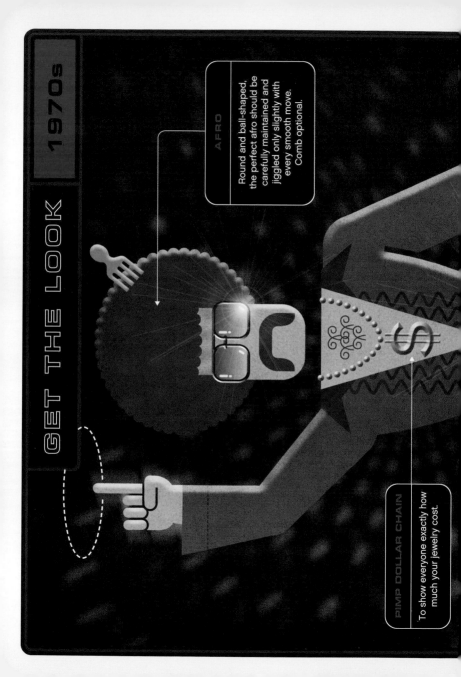

GET THE LOOK

AFRO

Round and ball-shaped, the perfect afro should be carefully maintained and jiggled only slightly with every smooth move. Comb optional.

PIMP DOLLAR CHAIN

To show everyone exactly how much your jewelry cost.

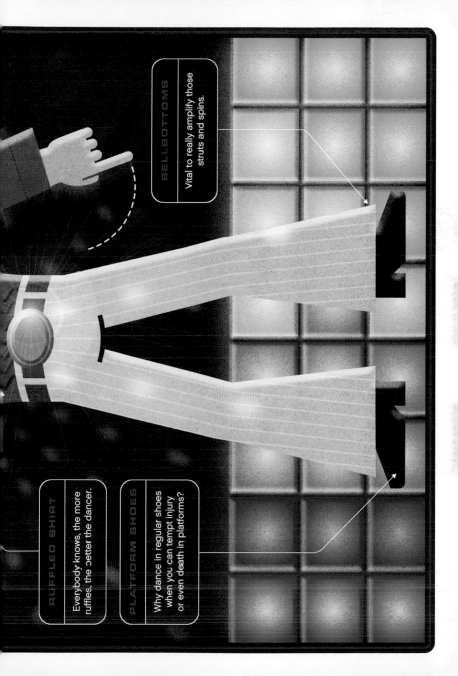

BELLBOTTOMS

Vital to really amplify those struts and spins.

RUFFLED SHIRT

Everybody knows, the more ruffles, the better the dancer.

PLATFORM SHOES

Why dance in regular shoes when you can tempt injury or even death in platforms?

∫ATURDAY NIGHT FEVER

1 Hit the dance floor with the Travolta Strut (see page 12): It's the only way to make sure all eyes are on you.

2 Correctly aligned shirt cuffs are vital from the outset. Raise your left hand to adjust your cuff before repeating with the other hand.

3 Next, warm up the crowd by pointing out a few hotties. Then move forward, stepping with the beat and performing the egg-beater as you go (see page 54).

4 Standing still, point to the heavens with your right arm and place your left hand on your hips. Quickly reverse the action and point with the other arm. Repeat. This move never gets old.

continued

There is no cooler dance sequence. If you're after some 1970s nostalgia then Saturday Night Fever is just what you need! Throw on the soundtrack from the movie for a good boogie session.

 When you're done pointing, straighten your right leg and turn your left to the side. Keep it bent and only rest on your toes. Point out to the side with your left arm and bring your right hand to your hips. Twiddle your fingers like you're the best bass player in town and shake those hips.

 Cross your arms and hold them out at chest height. Now, drop to the ground by bending in your knees before shooting straight back up again. Repeat (assuming you're still able to move, of course.)

ESSENTIAL SOUNDS OF THE 1970s

- **Boogie Fever**
  The Sylvers

- **Heaven Must be Missing an Angel**
  Tavares

- **You Make Me Feel Like Dancing**
  Leo Sayer

- **Ladies Night**
  Kool and The Gang

- **Stayin' Alive**
  Bee Gees

- **The Hustle**
  Van McCoy and The Soul City Symphony

- **Last Dance**
  Donna Summer

- **YMCA**
  The Village People

- **Blame it on the Boogie**
  Jackson Five

- **Layla**
  Eric Clapton

- **Dancing Queen**
  Abba

- **Detroit Rock City**
  Kiss

- **Highway to Hell**
  AC/DC

- **Paranoid**
  Black Sabbath

- **More Than a Feeling**
  Boston

- **You Make Me Feel (Mighty Real)**
  Sylvester

- **Backstabbers**
  The O'Jays

- **Bad Company**
  Bad Company

- **The Boys Are Back in Town**
  Thin Lizzy

- **School's Out**
  Alice Cooper

- **T.N.T.**
  AC/DC

- **Our House**
  Crosby, Stills, Nash & Young

- **No Woman, No Cry**
  Bob Marley & The Wailers

- **Ballroom Blitz**
  Sweet

- **Sweet Home Alabama**
  Lynyrd Skynyrd

- **Barracuda**
  Heart

- **I Feel Love**
  Donna Summer

- **Night Fever**
  Bee Gees

- **Lady**
  Styx

- **Smoke on the Water**
  Deep Purple

- **White Riot**
  The Clash

- **Stir It Up**
  Bob Marley & The Wailers

- **You Really Got Me**
  Van Halen

- **Video Killed the Radio Star**
  The Buggles

- **Rapper's Delight**
  The Sugarhill Gang

- **No More Mr. Nice Guy**
  Alice Cooper

- **Get Up (I Feel Like Being A) Sex Machine**
  James Brown

- **Le Freak**
  Chic

- **Boogie Wonderland**
  Earth, Wind & Fire

19

80s

The era of electro beats, New Wave chic, and pop rock treats, the sounds of the 1980s are big and bold. Strap on your sneakers and prepare to rock the dance floor.

- THE TIMEWARP
- MOONWALK
- BREAKDANCE
- THE ROBOT

The

WANNA DANCE LIKE THEY DID IN THE 80s? It's easy, just think big—in fact the bigger the better. It was a decade of ostentatious individualism, and the music and dance scenes were no exception, from electro beats to synthesized harmonies. Loyal subjects of the King of Pop himself had plenty to dance about and for everyone else, the 80s were never short of dance tracks. Read on for the key tunes, scenes, and players to get you in the mood to dance the night away.

KING OF THE MOVES

Probably the most famous pop icon ever. Michael Jackson not only stole the 80s music scene, he changed dance forever. No one could move, spin, or throw a hat like him. As well as classic tracks like "Thriller," "Bad," and "Billy Jean," Jacko gave us countless moves to truly impress on the dance floor, from the Moonwalk to the crotch hold. And of course the legendary exclamation, "Oww!," with which to finish any 80s dance move.

MUSICAL TV

With the launch of MTV in 1981, lavish music videos began to have a huge effect on the record industry. The first video aired was "Video Killed the Radio Star" by The Buggles.

A DANCER'S PARADISE

A Parisian dance haven, Les Bain-Douches was actually opened in the late 70s but came to prominence during the following decade. Phillipe Starck started his interior design career by sprucing up the old Turkish baths and creating this wonderful dance arena. The crème de la crème of celeb society graced its floors and it's still a dance Mecca today.

ESSENTIAL LYRICS

"You know that we are living in a material world / And I am a material girl."

Madonna hit the music scene in the early 80s and quickly became the poster girl for 80s pop. The dance floor filler "Material Girl" (1985) was one of her most iconic songs, capturing the consumerist culture of the decade. Madonna has since claimed that she would never have recorded the song had she known that its title would become her long-running nickname.

ALT SCENE

Not so keen on pure pop? Try New Wave, the 80s alternative, often described as "polished Punk." Artists included The Police, Blondie, and No Doubt, among many others.

BODYPOPPING

Bodypopping, like other forms of breakdancing, arose from the NY street dance scene of the late 70s and early 80s. Poppers jerk different parts of their body by contracting and relaxing various muscles.

THE
TIME WARP

1 You can't go wrong with this classic sequence, just listen to the lyrics and follow the steps. First jump to the left with your feet together.

2 Follow this with a step to the right. Throw in a little sway as you go if you've got this mastered.

3 Place both hands on your hips, and bring your knees in together. You should look like you need the bathroom.

4 Thrust your pelvis forward and back before spinning your hips. Repeat to the beat until the track ends. Let's do the Time Warp again!

Debuting in The Rocky Horror Picture Show *stage show in 1973, this dance number really hit the big time in the 80s, with the cult film of the same name doing brisk business around the world. It's easy to dance like a Transylvanian—just shed your dignity and start thrusting.*

MOONWALK

1 No, not the clumsy, slow steps of Neil Armstrong. This is the backward glide immortalized by the late, great Michael Jackson. To start, bend your right knee and place the ball of your right foot behind you. Keep your left leg straight.

2 Using your right foot as a base, drag your left leg back behind you on the ball of your heel, keeping it straight. Your right foot stays where it is. Stick your head out like it's being left behind.

3 As you stop your left leg, bring the heel of your right snapping down while simultaneously snapping your left heel up, thereby switching your leg positions. Smooth.

4 Continue the slide by repeating these steps and alternating your legs. Add arm movements by bringing your right arm back as you drag your left leg back and then do the same for the right leg.

This was the King of Pop's signature move. The inspiration for this iconic dance finds its roots in the work of the famous mime artist Marcel Marceau. If you can pull this one off, you'll be king of the dance floor wherever you bust it.

BREAK-DANCE

1 This one ain't for the faint-hearted. To start, you need to get in a position like you're about to do a press up. Your arms should be straight, shoulder-width apart, with your palms on the floor. Your legs should be straight and aligned with your arms.

2 Straighten and raise your left arm at a slight angle above you and bring your right leg underneath your left leg. Lift your left foot onto the toes, and rest your right foot on the side of the foot.

3 Now, bring your left leg forward behind your right knee. Bend your right knee at the same time and transfer your weight to your right arm. Your legs should now be crossed a little.

4 Transfer your weight to your left leg, uncross your legs and adopt the crab position, with your body facing upward supported by your arms underneath you.

continued

5 Shift your balance to your left hand, cross your left leg over your right one, and raise your right arm.

6 Gradually put your weight on your left leg by pushing down on your inner sole and extend your right left backward. You should now mirror step 2.

7 Lower your right arm to the floor as you pull your left leg back under you. You should now be back at step 1.

8 Repeat the sequence, getting quicker and quicker the more confident you get. You'll be winning your breakdance battles in no time!

Super cool DJs who were breaking beats and laying down samples created a new sound that inspired this new dance revolution. Emanating from the urban hip hop scene of the 80s, the trend has never looked back, continuing to thrive throughout the 90s, and as popular today as ever.

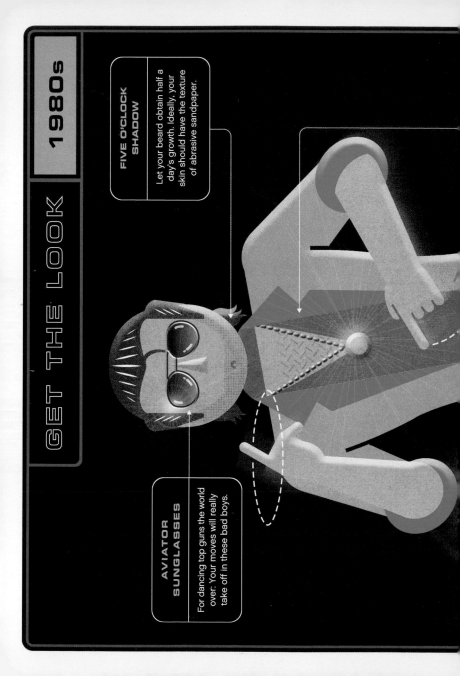

1980s

FIVE O'CLOCK SHADOW

Let your beard obtain half a day's growth. Ideally, your skin should have the texture of abrasive sandpaper.

AVIATOR SUNGLASSES

For dancing top guns the world over: Your moves will really take off in these bad boys.

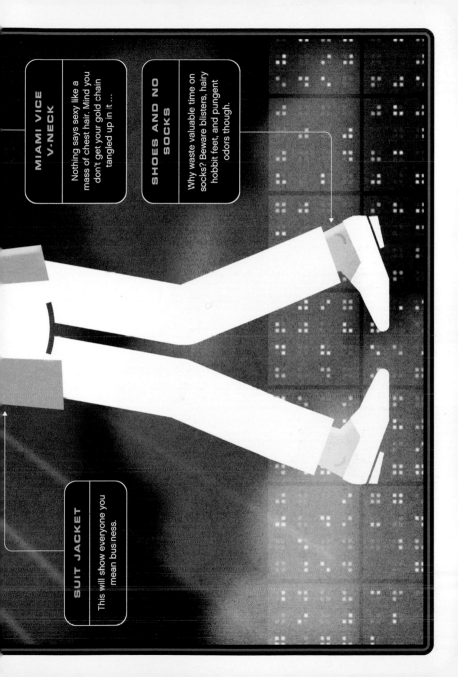

MIAMI VICE V-NECK

Nothing says sexy like a mass of chest hair. Mind you don't get your gold chain tangled up in it....

SHOES AND NO SOCKS

Why waste valuable time on socks? Beware blisters, hairy hobbit feet, and pungent odors though.

SUIT JACKET

This will show everyone you mean business.

THE
ROBOT

1 Initiate dance sequence . . . Imagine all your joints have frozen, lock your shoulders, and slowly raise your forearms to waist height, palms facing each other.

2 Next, turn your head to the left before twisting the top half of your body to the left. Lower your left arm and raise your right arm a few times. That's it, do the bionic boogie.

3 Halt like you've received a new command and in one fluid motion put your arms back into position one and turn your body to the right.

4 Now start to walk with straight legs: As you step with your right, move your right arm out and vice versa. Who's the Groovatron!

continued

The world famous Robot was created by Charles Washington in 1960, though it really took off on mainstream dance floors in the 80s. Part of the popping and locking street dance scenes that began in the late 1970s, it's about contracting and relaxing muscles in time to the beat for a funky, jerky movement.

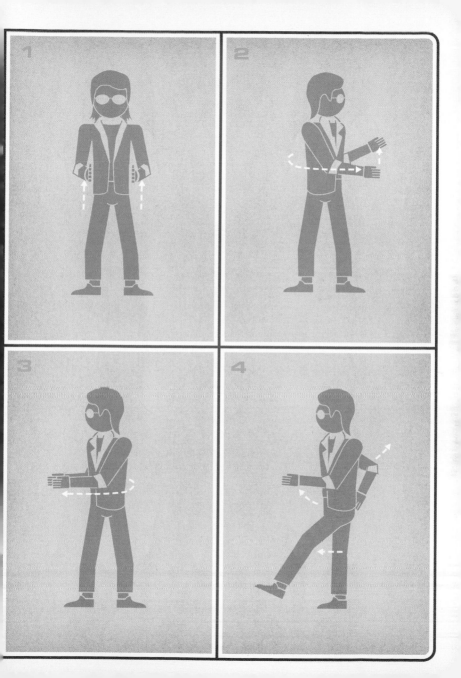

 Jolt to a stop. Bend your arms at the elbows slightly and position your hands in front of your hips, palms open. Now move them jerkily, in and out, while also jerking your head from side to side.

Keep this movement going and start to move from side to side by swiveling your lead foot on your toes and heel and dragging your other foot. Think of yourself as a zombie robot.

ESSENTIAL SOUNDS OF THE 1980s

- **Bust A Move**
  Young MC

- **Billie Jean**
  Michael Jackson

- **Beat It**
  Michael Jackson

- **When Doves Cry**
  Prince

- **Push It**
  Salt-N-Pepa

- **Flashdance...What a Feeling**
  Irene Cara

- **It's Raining Men**
  The Weather Girls

- **Holiday**
  Madonna

- **Thriller**
  Michael Jackson

- **I'm So Excited**
  The Pointer Sisters

- **Electric Slide**
  Marcia Griffiths

- **I'm Coming Out**
  Diana Ross

- **Bad**
  Michael Jackson

- **Walking On Sunshine**
  Katrina and The Waves

- **Pump Up the Jam**
  Technotronic feat. Felly

- **Fame (I Want To Live Forever)**
  Irene Cara

- **I Wanna Dance With Somebody (Who Loves Me)**
  Whitney Houston

- **Dancing on the Ceiling**
  Lionel Richie

- **Relax (Don't Do It)**
  Frankie Goes To Hollywood

- **You Spin Me Round (Like a Record)**
  Dead or Alive

- **She Works Hard For the Money**
  Donna Summer

- **Papa Don't Preach**
  Madonna

- **Take on Me**
  a-ha

- **Walk Like An Egyptian**
  The Bangles

- **Call Me**
  Blondie

- **(Let's Get) Physical**
  Olivia Newton John

- **Girls Just Wanna Have Fun**
  Cyndi Lauper

- **Let's Dance**
  David Bowie

- **Come On Eileen**
  Dexy's Midnight Runners and Emerald Express

- **Smooth Criminal**
  Michael Jackson

- **Electric Avenue**
  Eddy Grant

- **Hungry Like The Wolf**
  Duran Duran

- **99 Red Balloons**
  Nena

- **Footloose**
  Kenny Loggins

- **Eye of the Tiger**
  Survivor

- **Wake Me Up Before You Go Go**
  Wham

- **Born in the USA**
  Bruce Springsteen

- **9-5**
  Dolly Parton

- **Ice Ice Baby**
  Vanilla Ice

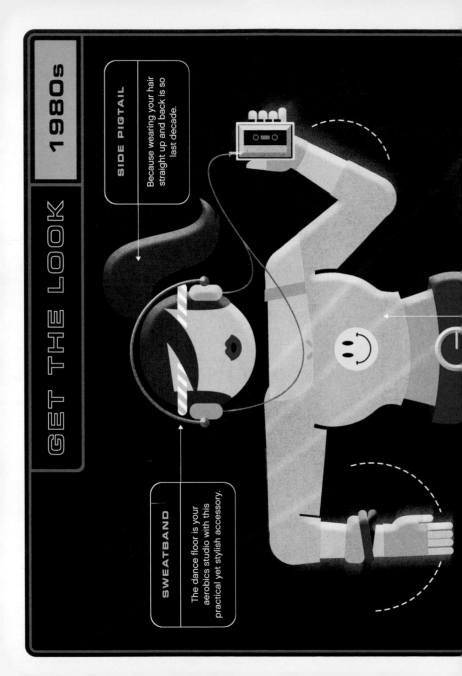

SIDE PIGTAIL

Because wearing your hair straight up and back is so last decade.

SWEATBAND

The dance floor is your aerobics studio with this practical yet stylish accessory.

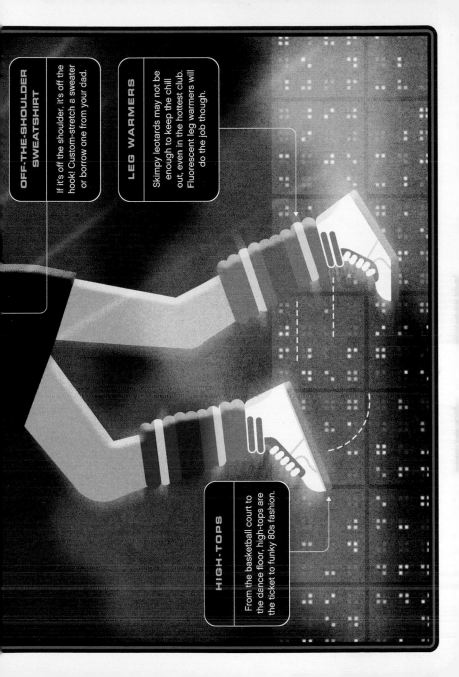

OFF-THE-SHOULDER SWEATSHIRT

If it's off the shoulder, it's off the hook! Custom-stretch a sweater or borrow one from your dad.

LEG WARMERS

Skimpy leotards may not be enough to keep the chill out, even in the hottest club. Fluorescent leg warmers will do the job though.

HIGH-TOPS

From the basketball court to the dance floor, high-tops are the ticket to funky 80s fashion.

19

90s

Possibly the most diverse decade in terms of dance floor hits, the 1990s had it all. From hip hop classics to pop platters and rock legends, it's time to get jiggy with it.

- HAPPY RAVER
- RUNNING MAN
- HAMMER DANCE
- THE MACARENA

The 1990s

THE 90s WAS A PHENOMENAL DECADE for dance lovers everywhere. Whether you feel like channeling your inner teeny-bopper, grunge rocker or hip hopper, there's plenty to get excited about. Super-groups like the Spice Girls, Backstreet Boys, and New Kids on the Block conquered the world with their bubblegum pop tunes and iconic dance routines, grunge rock reached a melancholy high with the likes of Nirvana, and hip hop hit the mainstream as Vanilla Ice and MC Hammer got everyone dancing to the inner city beats. Strap on your sneakers and pull up your hammer pants, this dance floor is about to hit the 90s.

MC HAMMER

The man who's so famous he has a type of pant named after him, MC Hammer helped bring hip hop into the mainstream for the first time. Not your average hip hop homey, Hammer added a bit of populist flare to an otherwise hard, urban scene. Everyone on the planet must have heard his all-time greatest track, "U Can't Touch This" (1990). It's the type of song that makes you drop everything just to drop a few moves. The music video featured some of the most celebrated dance moves ever. And, of course, those pants.

RAVE ON

The late 80s and early 90s witnessed the birth of an underground movement dedicated to dance. Across the world, in fields and warehouses, people gathered to dance the night away. These free parties attracted huge numbers, with regular attendance topping five figures. Raves offered many styles of music, from acid house to jungle, happy hardcore, techno, and trance.

TEENYBOPPING

Bubblegum pop was massive in the 90s, and one of the biggest pop groups was the Spice Girls. People couldn't get enough of their catchy tracks in clubs around the world. Their songs ranged from the up-tempo, hit-the-dance-floor-podium variety, to the smooth and sultry, perfect-for-slow-dancing kind. "Wannabe" (1996) was their first smash-hit record and sold over 6 million copies worldwide, topping the charts in 31 countries. It was the biggest song of the decade and is a definite dance floor filler wherever it's played.

BIRTH OF BRITPOP

Intended as a response to the predominance of US grunge, the rise of Britpop saw bands such as Oasis, Blur, and Pulp achieve global success with their uniquely British sounds, catchy hooks, and relevant lyrics. Part of a wider cultural movement named Cool Britannia, by the end of the decade the Britpop scene had largely burned out.

THE SEATTLE SOUND

Who could forget the long, unkempt hair, hardy outdoor shoes, lumberjack shirts, and ripped jeans that defined the grunge rock movement? These guys were downbeat and down with the masses. Nirvana and Pearl Jam were the leaders of this music revolution that saw melancholy melodies and rocking guitar riffs take center stage.

HAPPY RAVER

1 Anything goes in the house of dance. Throw your arms in the air and wave them around like you just don't care. Sprinkle some fairy dust while you're at it . . . feel the magic.

2 Show off some big fish-little fish action by tucking in your elbows by your sides, extending your palms, and stretching out your forearms. Move your hands in and out.

3 Do the cardboard box: turn your arms 90 degrees so that your left arm is above your right. Push them in and out, switch them over, then rotate them back and work the sides.

4 Now jump up and down with one hand in the air. Point to the DJ as you jump, and show him some love!

The early 90s was the era of the rave junkie. These routines are just a few examples of the crazy moves you can bust to all types of dance music. Why not also try stacking some shelves or drying yourself off with a towel? Household routines are never this much fun in real life.

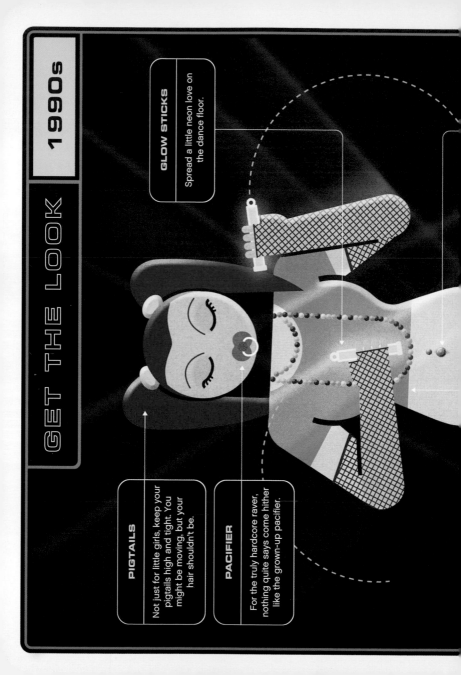

GLOW STICKS

Spread a little neon love on the dance floor.

PIGTAILS

Not just for little girls, keep your pigtails high and tight. You might be moving, but your hair shouldn't be.

PACIFIER

For the truly hardcore raver, nothing quite says come hither like the grown-up pacifier.

BELLY-BUTTON PIERCING

Why stop at the ears? Belly-button rings and crop tops – a match made in heaven.

CROP TOP

Because a whole T-shirt is way too extravagant. Cut down on the needless waste of fabric adopt the crop top.

COMBAT PANTS

A dance floor can be a bit like a war zone. Loud noises, people screaming, and break-dance battles. Be prepared; wear some combats.

GET THE LOOK

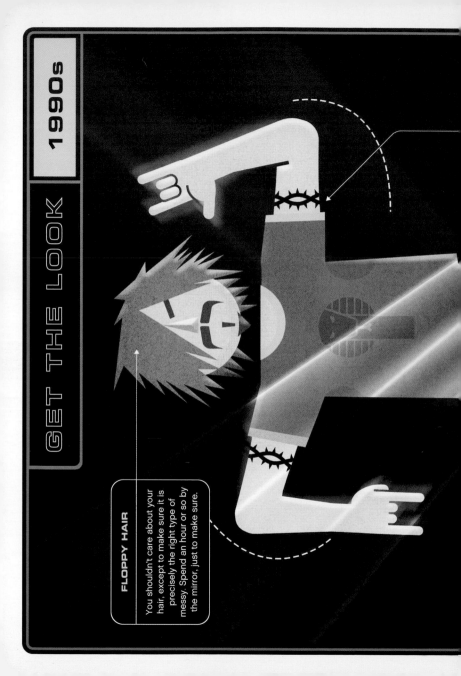

FLOPPY HAIR

You shouldn't care about your hair, except to make sure it is precisely the right type of messy. Spend an hour or so by the mirror, just to make sure.

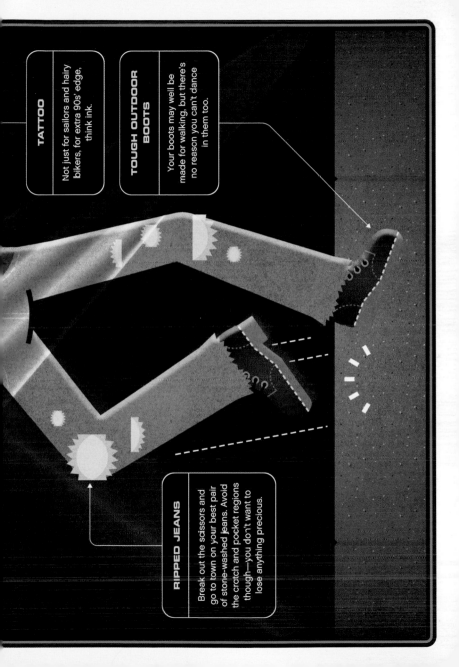

TATTOO

Not just for sailors and hairy bikers, for extra 90s' edge, think ink.

TOUGH OUTDOOR BOOTS

Your boots may well be made for walking, but there's no reason you can't dance in them too.

RIPPED JEANS

Break out the scissors and go to town on your best pair of stone-washed jeans. Avoid the crotch and pocket regions though—you don't want to lose anything precious.

RUNNING MAN

1 The name may say "man," but this move is for anyone who's got the groove. Raise your right leg and bend your knee to 90 degrees. Keep your left leg straight. Raise your arms straight out in front of you.

2 Slam that right leg back down to the ground as you slide your left leg backward. Bring your elbows down to your side at the same time.

3 Repeat this movement using alternate legs, and keep on running on the same spot.

4 After four jogs, turn on your heel and face the other way but keep on running like your life depends on it. Exercise never looked so good.

Paula Abdul created this little number for Janet Jackson in the late 1980s, though it was MC Hammer who went on to really make the move his own in the early 90s.

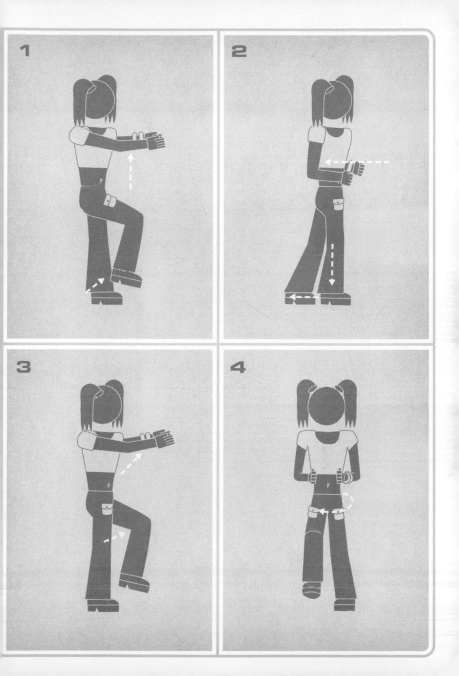

HAMMER DANCE

1. Raise both arms to shoulder height and stick out your elbows and knees shoulder-width apart. Lift your left elbow slightly and at the same time, stretch out your right arm and bend your right knee in. Hammer Time!

2. Do the Running Man (see page 98). A pair of baggy hammer pants can only improve the effect of this dance.

3. With your arms and elbows pointed out, jump up, bending your knees.

4. As you land, cross your legs and spin around, uncrossing your legs as you come around to face the front again.

continued

5 If you're limber enough, lean backward with your right arm stretched out behind you. Bend your knees and arch your back as you lean backward. Once your hand hits the floor, push off and straighten your legs to stand up again. You may not want to try this one without on-hand medical assistance.

6 On the spot, criss-cross your legs really quickly and then jump with knees bent.

7 Bend your legs so your knees are pointing out to the sides. Place your hands on your hips, elbows pointing out. Swivel your lead foot to propel yourself across the floor, dragging your left leg as you go. Try it both ways.

This one-man dance machine hit the big time in the late 80s and early 90s. Real name Stanley Kirk Burrell, MC Hammer is considered a dance legend and you can see why. His rise and fall from fame was as dramatic as his moves, and after a turbulent time in the late 90s he became a preacher. Occasionally he does still dance.

THE
MACARENA

1 Time for some cheese. Raise your right arm to shoulder height palm down, and then raise your left arm alongside. Flip your palms over, one at a time, so they face up.

2 Bring each hand up to the opposite shoulder, right then left, so your arms are crossing.

3 Raise your right hand to your right ear, then the left to your left ear. Anyone else gone deaf?

4 Next, bring your right arm down to your left hip and your left arm down to your right hip, so that your arms are crossed again.

continued

Did you know this one-hit wonder is one of the best-selling songs of all time? At its zenith people all over the world danced the Macarena, including a President and 50,000 NY Yankees fans during a game.

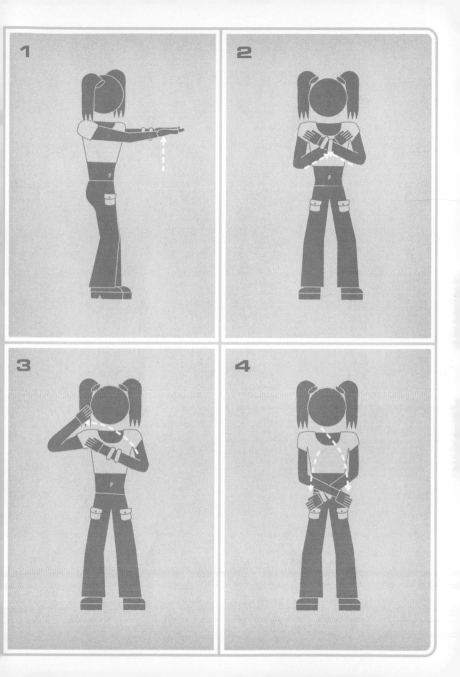

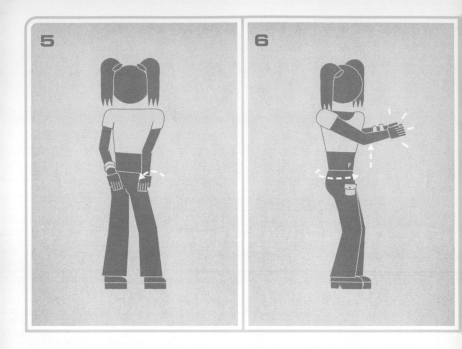

5 Bring your left hand to your left buttock followed by your right hand to your right buttock. Mighty fine rump!

6 Spin your hips once, then jump, turning 90 degrees in the air. Finish the move with a handclap. Repeat until the music abates. Ideally this should be performed with a cast of thousands.

ESSENTIAL SOUNDS OF THE 1990s

- **Vogue**
  Madonna

- **The Power**
  SNAP!

- **Baby Got Back**
  Sir Mix-A-Lot

- **Whoomp! There It Is**
  Tag Team

- **Unbelievable**
  EMF

- **U Can't Touch This**
  MC Hammer

- **Gettin' Jiggy Wit It**
  Will Smith

- **Believe (Life After Love)**
  Cher

- **Touch Me (All Night Long)**
  Cathy Dennis

- **Rhythm is a Dancer**
  SNAP!

- **Children (Dream version)**
  Robert Miles

- **Summertime**
  DJ Jazzy Jeff & The Fresh Prince

- **It's Like That '98**
  Jason Nevins vs Run-D.M.C.

- **Wannabe**
  Spice Girls

- **Girls and Boys**
  Blur

- **Macarena**
  Los Del Rio

- **Baby One More Time**
  Britney Spears

- **I'm Too Sexy**
  Right Said Fred

- **Here Comes the Hotstepper (Heartical mix)**
  Ini Kamoze

- **Everybody's Free (To Feel Good)**
  Rozalla

- **I Like To Move It**
  Real 2 Real feat. The Mad Stuntman

- **This Is How We Do It**
  Montell Jordan

- **Jump Around**
  House of Pain

- **Achy Breaky Heart**
  Billy Ray Cyrus

- **Jump**
  Kris Kross

- **Oh Carolina**
  Shaggy

- **Go**
  Moby

- **Black Or White**
  Michael Jackson

- **Around the World**
  Daft Punk

- **Mo Money, Mo Problems**
  Notorious BIG feat. Puff Daddy & Ma$e

- **Blue (Da Ba Dee)**
  Eiffel 65

- **Livin' La Vida Loca**
  Ricky Martin

- **Kernkraft 400**
  Zombie Nation

- **The Rockafeller Skank**
  Fatboy Slim

- **No Limit**
  2 Unlimited

- **Scatman (Ski Ba Bop Ba Dop Bop)**
  Scatman John

- **Firestarter**
  The Prodigy

- **Kiss Them For Me**
  Siouxsie and the Banshees

- **What Is Love**
  Haddaway

20

00s

A new millennium can only mean one thing—time to party! Heralding a decade of new musical twists on old soulful sounds, the 2000s is where it's at when it comes to burning up the dance floor.

- HIP HOP STOMP
- BOOTY SHAKE
- CRANKING
- AIR GUITAR

The

2000s

THE BRAVE NEW WORLD of the 21st century kept the dance traditions of old burning brightly. The last decade has seen offerings from dance legends Madonna and Kylie sounding and looking fresher than ever and has also given rise to major comebacks from some of the hottest artists from decades past. That's not to say there weren't also plenty of new musical marvels. Electro went big across Europe and emo was massive across the world. Sythpop, new wave, post-punk, R'n'B, crunk—the list of dance floor favorites is endless.

KEEPING IT REAL

This was the decade of the reality star. Whether singing or dancing, many of the huge hits of the 2000s got their big break via TV. Shows like *American Idol*, *Pop Idol*, and *X Factor* were and still are a massive commercial success story and the formats have been sold the world over. A whole host of dance shows also hit the small screen and many became global phenomena. *So You Think You Can Dance?* Read on to discover some of the greatest moves of the century!

KING OF THE MOVES

From the heavily strummed guitar intro to the funky drum beat, Justin Timberlake's first solo single, "Like I Love You" (2002), is a great dance floor track. A sparse but effective arrangement, its creative sampling of classic tracks are sure to get you going. Don't forget to check out Justin's own super-smooth moves for added inspiration.

DANCE SENSATIONS

The first decade of the 21st century saw the emergence of a fresh batch of new dance stars perfectly prepared to wow the world with their talents. Usher, Britney Spears, Christina Aguilera, and Rihanna were just some of the artists who kept people on the dance floor with their slick routines and original moves. The movie world got in on the dance act with box office bonanzas in the form of *High School Musical* and *Hairspray*—perfect sources for dance inspiration.

SUPER CLUB

London's Fabric was the superclub of the 00s and remains one of the greatest dance venues in the world. Opened in 1999, it's still the global mecca for lovers of electronic dance music, hip hop, and break beats as well as emerging new musical talent from around the world. The ultimate dance experience for hardcore clubbers.

CRANK THAT SOUND UP

Feeling like hip hop is just so last century? You need crunk. Originating in the southern states of America, crunk holds many of the elements of classic hip hop but is generally slower in tempo and focuses more on catchy beats and lyrics that you'll remember. It's a party sound designed to get you dancing and shouting out loud rather than slow dancing with your dad.

HIP HOP STOMP

1 Kick out your right leg and stomp, then kick out your left leg and stomp. Repeat but this time kick out twice both times before stomping.

2 Do the muscle: Clench your fist, bend your arm and swing it into your body, before bending down a little and pumping your arm down. Repeat with your left.

3 Clap your hands high above your head four times and fast with the beat.

4 Finally, rock your shoulders forward and back four times before closing with a "cut" motion to your neck. It's a wrap!

This hip hop move has its roots in Atlanta, the home town of Usher, Ludacris, and Lil Jon, who made this sequence famous in their track "Yeah!" (2004).

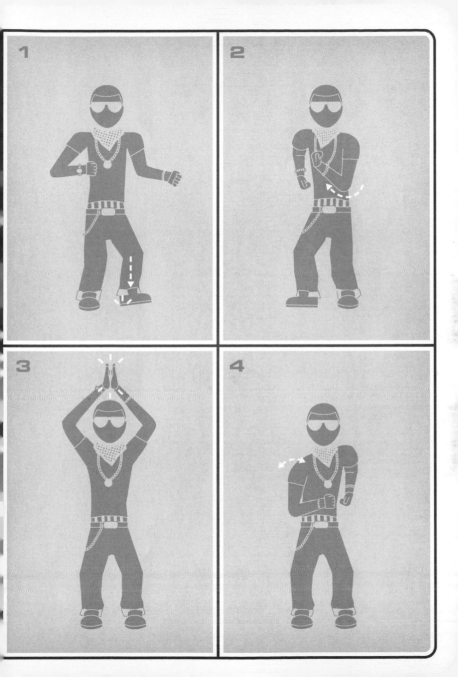

BOOTY SHAKE

1   Not just for ladies, guys: Master this move and strike a blow for sex equality. Stand with your legs shoulder-width apart and bend your legs slightly. Raise your arms up to your chest, stick your elbows out, and clench your fists.

2   With the first beat jump forward slightly, barely raising your feet off the ground.

3   As you land, push your elbows out sideways and your chest forward. As the top half of your body moves out, push your hips and booty back.

4   Now bring your arms back in, close to your chest, and thrust your hips forward. Repeat over and over, shuffling forward a little as you go. Go on, shake that butt.

To be a real 2000s dance floor diva, you have to break out the Booty Shake. And who better to turn to than Beyoncé when it comes to seeking inspiration for this bad ass move. If you need a tune to shake it to, crank up the volume on her classic "Crazy In Love" (2003).

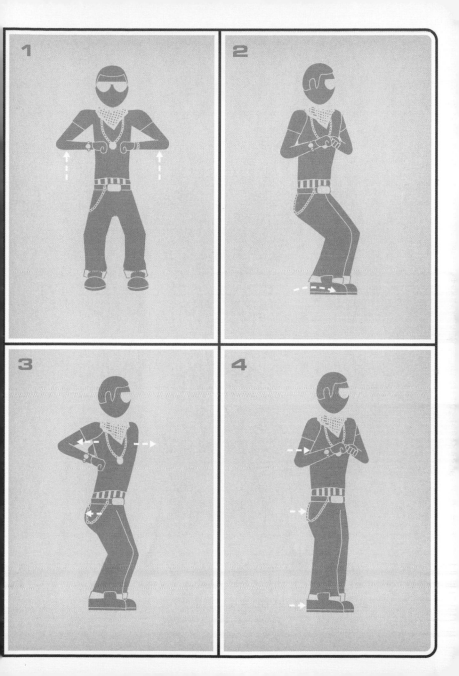

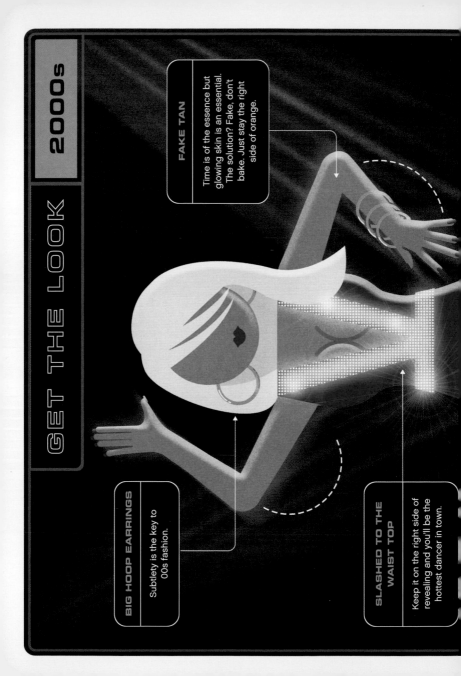

GET THE LOOK

FAKE TAN

Time is of the essence but glowing skin is an essential. The solution? Fake, don't bake. Just stay the right side of orange.

BIG HOOP EARRINGS

Subtlety is the key to 00s fashion.

SLASHED TO THE WAIST TOP

Keep it on the right side of revealing and you'll be the hottest dancer in town.

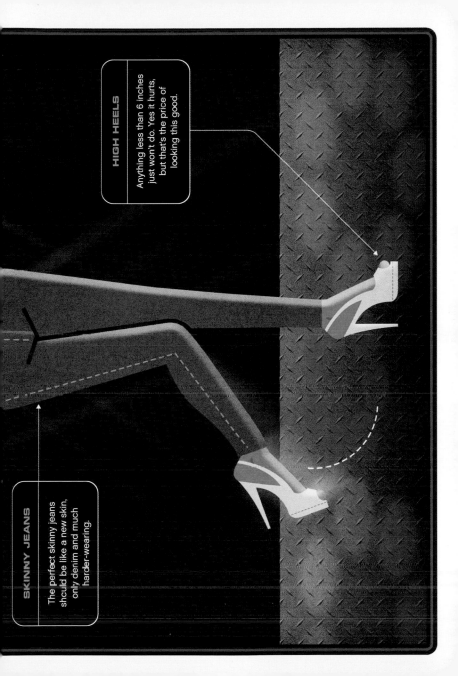

HIGH HEELS

Anything less than 6 inches just won't do. Yes it hurts, but that's the price of looking this good.

SKINNY JEANS

The perfect skinny jeans should be like a new skin, only denim and much harder-wearing.

CRANKING

1 Time to crank that soulja up. As the music starts, jump up slightly and cross your legs as you land, with your left foot behind your back.

2 Jump straight back to your starting position, uncrossing your legs. Bend your elbows by your sides with your forearms stretched out in front of you, palms facing forward.

3 Raise your left leg up behind you so it crosses your body and touch your heel with your right hand. Make sure you keep your balance— falling over is most definitely not cool. Bring your foot back to the floor.

4 Bend your legs slightly and put your weight on your right foot. Punch out with your right hand, then with your left before stamping your left leg down lightly on your toes.

continued

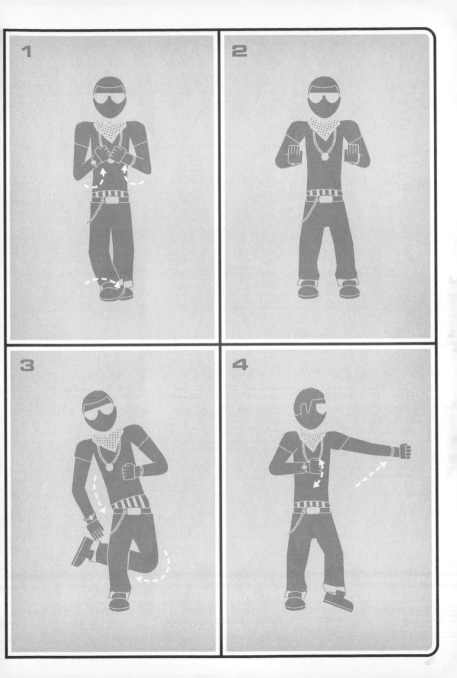

Transfer your weight to the left leg and lower your body. Tuck your arms in, with your palms facing the floor. Cross your right leg over your left, stamping it down lightly on your toes.

 In quick time, bring your right leg back to the starting position, stamping down lightly on your toes again. Pretend you're stamping on egg shells and trying not to break them.

 Raise your right leg up to your waist and hit your thigh. Not some corny folk dance slap; keep it real with hip hop cool. Avoid doing any permanent damage though.

8 Standing on your right leg, stick your left leg out behind and lean forward. Raise both arms out to the side and stretched slightly behind you and do the Superman. Forget Clark Kent, you're an inner-city superhuman dance machine, born to boogie.

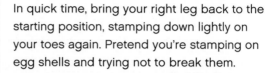

For true hip hop hipsters, cranking is a must. "Crank That" by Soulja Boy (2007) is the inspiration for these moves. If it's good enough for 5 million internet viewers, it should be good enough for you!

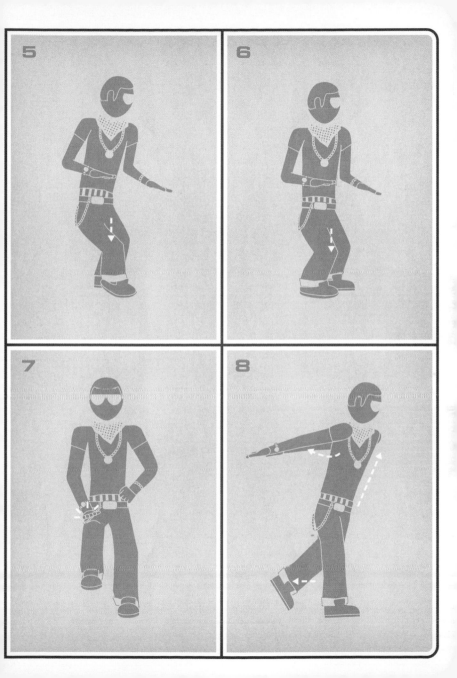

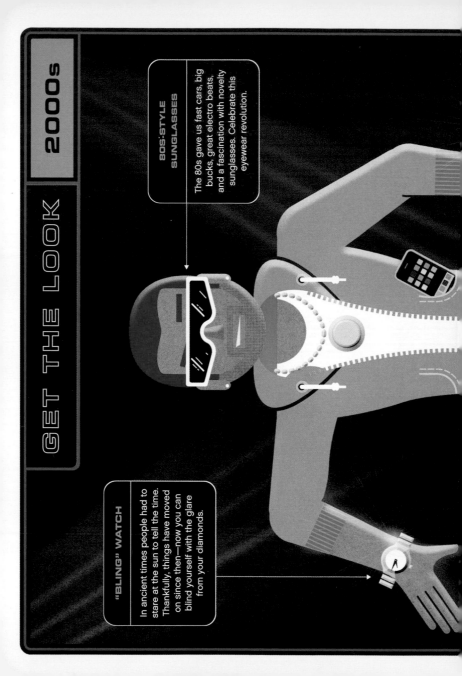

GET THE LOOK

80s-STYLE SUNGLASSES

The 80s gave us fast cars, big bucks, great electro beats, and a fascination with novelty sunglasses. Celebrate this eyewear revolution.

"BLING" WATCH

In ancient times people had to stare at the sun to tell the time. Thankfully, things have moved on since then—now you can blind yourself with the glare from your diamonds.

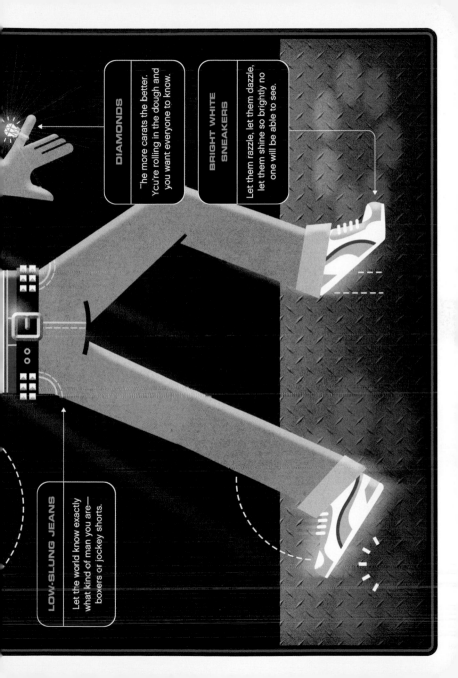

DIAMONDS

The more carats the better. You're rolling in the dough and you want everyone to know.

BRIGHT WHITE SNEAKERS

Let them razzle, let them dazzle, let them shine so brightly no one will be able to see.

LOW-SLUNG JEANS

Let the world know exactly what kind of man you are—boxers or jockey shorts.

AIR GUITAR

1 To start, switch on your imagination. Sure you may not look the part but you're a rock god, with a stadium full of fans. Hit them with a windmill by holding the neck of your air guitar as you would a real one, with your left hand. Swing your fully extended right arm in large circles, strumming the chord each time.

2 A quick serenade is in order. Get down on one knee, rest your "guitar" on your knee, and strum away.

3 Stand side-on and lower and raise your front shoulder to the beat. If you want to go crowd-surfing at this point, no one's going to stop you.

4 Use your leg as a guitar: Raise your left leg out in front of you (as straight as possible). Hold the ankle-end like you're playing the chord and strum your thigh. Hop along as you go for added effect.

continued

5 No air guitar solo is complete without the forward skid. Take a short run up, fall to your knees, and with the momentum, slide forward.

6 End by going crazy and smashing the guitar. Any solid object will do: Floor, wall, wardrobe. Don't worry, you won't damage anything—it isn't real.

....

Historically the domain of inebriated uncles at a wedding, Air Guitar is now an acceptable form of dance . . . sort of. There is even a World Championship in the discipline. So get practicing.

ESSENTIAL SOUNDS OF THE 2000s

- **Umbrella**
  Rihanna featuring Jay Z

- **Don't' Cha**
  Pussycat Dolls

- **Cha Cha Slide**
  DJ Casper

- **Get Low**
  Lil Jon and the East Side Boyz

- **Crank That**
  Soulja Boy

- **Candyman**
  Chrisina Aguilera

- **The Ketchup Song**
  Las Ketchup

- **Let's Get it Started**
  Black Eyed Peas

- **Yeah!**
  Usher featuring Lil' Jon and Ludacris

- **Who Let The Dogs Out**
  Baha Men

- **Hot in Here**
  Nelly

- **Work It**
  Missy Elliot

- **Clocks**
  Coldplay

- **Hung Up**
  Madonna

- **Lose Yourself**
  Eminem

- **Sounds of the Underground**
  Girls Aloud

- **Beautiful Girls**
  Sean Kingston

- **Dance, Dance**
  Fallout Boy

- **I Believe In A Thing Called Love**
  The Darkness

- **Get The Party Started**
  Pink

- **Last Night**
  The Strokes

- **Take Me Out**
  Franz Ferdinand

- **Crazy In Love**
  Beyonce featuring Jay Z

- **The Reason**
  Hoobastank

- **I See You Baby**
  Groove Armada

- **In Da Club**
  50 Cent

- **I Predict a Riot**
  Kaiser Chiefs

- **Just Dance**
  Lady Gaga

- **Genie In A Bottle**
  Christina Aguilera

- **Like I Love You**
  Justin Timberlake

- **Gold Digger**
  Kanye West

- **Hips Don't Lie**
  Shakira

- **It's My Life**
  No Doubt

- **Independent Woman**
  Destiny's Child

- **Hey Ya!**
  Outkast

- **SexyBack**
  Justin Timberlake

- **Hollaback Girl**
  Gwen Stefani

- **Toxic**
  Britney Spears

- **Can't Get You Out of My Head**
  Kylie Minogue

- **I Kissed A Girl**
  Katy Perry

INDEX